VANESSA FELTZ

The Unfiltered Memoir of an Amazing Journalist

Olivia Stevenson

Copyright © 2024 Olivia Stevenson.

All rights reserved. This work is protected by copyright law and may not be reproduced, distributed, transmitted, displayed, published, or broadcast without the prior written permission of the copyright owner. You may not alter or remove any trademark, copyright, or other notice from copies of the content. Unauthorized use and/or duplication of this material without express and written permission from the copyright owner is strictly prohibited. Excerpts and links may be used, provided that full and clear credit is given to Olivia Stevenson with appropriate and specific direction to the original content.

TABLE OF CONTENTS

INTRODUCTION — 5

CHAPTER ONE — 11
Early Life and Inspirations — *11*

CHAPTER TWO — 21
The Rise of a Journalist — *21*

CHAPTER THREE — 31
From Print to Screen — *31*

CHAPTER FOUR — 41
Vanessa the Person — *41*

CHAPTER FIVE — 51
A Voice for Many — *51*

CHAPTER SIX   **61**

   Criticism and Resilience   *61*

CHAPTER SEVEN   **71**

   A Legacy Beyond Journalism   *71*

CONCLUSION   **80**

INTRODUCTION

Few people are able to make a lasting impression on the public's mind in the dynamic world of media, where celebrities come and go, like Vanessa Feltz. Known for her unwavering sincerity, quick wit, and intelligence, Vanessa has amassed a career spanning over three decades and is now well-known throughout the United Kingdom. She is an indestructible force in British broadcasting. Vanessa's career is one of resiliency, reinvention, and breaking down boundaries, beginning with her early days as a print journalist and continuing through her move into radio and television. Her narrative is much more than just a record of her career accomplishments; it is a tribute to her inner strength, the value of self-belief, and the transforming force of remaining true to oneself in a field where superficiality is all too common.

Vanessa was raised in a very different environment from the glitzy celebrity world she would eventually occupy— Islington, London, was her birthplace. Her upbringing was marked by a strong emphasis on the importance of culture, education, and information. Vanessa showed early intelligence and an unquenchable curiosity, traits that would be crucial to her success in the future. But even with her apparent skills, Vanessa's ascent to the top of the British media landscape wasn't easy. Being a woman—particularly a Jewish woman—in a field controlled by men, Vanessa encountered racism and other challenges. She didn't let those obstacles stop her, though; instead, it gave her more motivation to disprove her critics.

Vanessa's life story is an inspiring illustration of someone who defied social pressure to conform. From her beginnings as a writer and columnist, where she developed her ability to write opinion pieces, to her ascent to fame on radio and television, Vanessa has continuously changed and never shied away from new chances or difficulties. Her move from print to television was especially impressive since it showed how she could change with the times without losing her distinctive style. Vanessa stood out from her peers with her direct, no-nonsense style of speaking on both serious political matters and lighter entertainment topics.

However, why is Vanessa's narrative important? In a society where the media is sometimes accused of encouraging conformity, superficiality, and exaggerated notions of success and beauty, Vanessa has always been a welcome diversion. She has been transparent about her problems with mental health, her issues with body image, and the difficulties of leading a public life that is closely watched. Vanessa has allowed people to be vulnerable by embracing her flaws and making them a part of her public persona rather than keeping them hidden. Vanessa is a well-liked figure that the public can relate to and trust in an industry that frequently values polish and precision.

As a trailblazer for women in journalism, Vanessa's impact is noteworthy in the most important ways. Vanessa fought for recognition during a period when women in broadcasting were frequently cast in less important positions. She didn't want to be just another "talking head"; instead, she wanted to use her platform to have important discussions, take on challenging topics, and, most importantly, be heard. By doing this, she opened the door for a new wave of female broadcasters and journalists to come after her.

But Vanessa's influence extends beyond her career successes. She also demonstrates personal resiliency in her experience. Vanessa's life was completely upended in 2000 when she and Michael Kurer went through a grueling and highly publicized divorce. Undoubtedly, Vanessa went through some of the most difficult periods of her life at this time, but she chose to use the experience to strengthen herself rather than let it define who she was. Vanessa has frequently discussed how, throughout that trying time, her profession gave her stability and a sense of purpose, and it also enabled her to find her own sense of self-worth and identity. She is a strong role model for others because of her openness about her personal challenges, which demonstrates to others that it is possible to endure hardship and emerge stronger on the other side.

A big part of Vanessa's legacy has also been her support of mental health awareness and body positivity. Vanessa has endured severe criticism about her appearance throughout her career, with tabloids usually focused on her weight rather than her accomplishments. Vanessa, however, has accepted her shape and utilized her platform to question society's limited notions of beauty, refusing to give in to pressure to fit in. Her candor regarding her personal weight loss experience, which included deciding to have gastric band surgery, has spurred crucial discussions about self-acceptance, body image, and the expectations placed on women in the public eye.

Apart from her career in the media, Vanessa's support of causes including mental health assistance, gender equality, and awareness of domestic abuse has had a lasting impression. The public discourse on problems that are frequently stigmatized or disregarded has become more compassionate and understanding as a result of her willingness to use her platform to address these challenges. Because of her personal experiences and her desire to improve the lives of others, Vanessa's advocacy is very personal. Her legacy is one of changing society overall, not just in the media. She has constantly utilized her voice to speak for others who might not have one.

Vanessa's impact is still very much there even as her career develops. There is no denying Vanessa's affinity for her audience, whether she is interacting with them on social media or hosting her well-liked BBC Radio 2 show. Her genuineness comes through in everything she does, and she has a remarkable capacity to make others feel heard and noticed. Vanessa's tale exemplifies perseverance, self-reinvention, and the bravery to be oneself in the face of difficulties or setbacks.

Through narrating Vanessa Feltz's secret narrative, this book aims to reveal the person behind the public image as well as the career high points. It's an exploration of the life of an extraordinary person whose impact goes well beyond the media landscape. Vanessa's story is important because it shows success in the face of hardship, shattering stereotypes and obstacles, and using one's position to change the world. Vanessa Feltz has made a lasting impact on British media and society by her work, campaigning, and personal tenacity. Her legacy will serve as an inspiration to future generations.

CHAPTER ONE

Early Life and Inspirations

On February 21, 1962, Vanessa Feltz was born into a middle-class Jewish family in Islington, London. When she was a child, Islington, a borough in North London noted for its historical significance and increasing affluence, was a vibrant and culturally diverse place. Even while Islington didn't have the glitzy exterior it would eventually acquire, it was still a bustling neighborhood in London that blended elements of developing middle-class sensibility with working-class roughness. Vanessa's upbringing in this place exposed her to a variety of customs, cultures, and social dynamics that influenced the way she saw the world.

Her mother, Valerie, was a homemaker who created a loving and intellectually stimulating atmosphere, while her father, Norman, was a prosperous lingerie manufacturer. Vanessa frequently describes her family as one that valued education and hard work, and where intellectual endeavors were encouraged from an early age. Despite their relative wealth, the Feltz family had strong Jewish roots and understood the value of morality, community, and compassion. This kind of upbringing would subsequently shape Vanessa's strong sense of social justice and her frequently daring approach to taking on challenges in her media career.

Vanessa was exposed to literature, current events, and debates at home from a young age since her parents valued education. Her father's business success instilled in her a strong work ethic and the belief that hard effort and perseverance might lead to success. Her family was never unduly lavish, even with their relatively decent financial circumstances, and they valued intellectual development over materialism.

In the 1960s and 1970s, Islington was a neighborhood undergoing change. Once a working-class neighborhood, it was gradually gentrifying and drawing a wider range of professionals, intellectuals, and artists. Vanessa's early years were set against a dynamic backdrop of old and modern, rich and poor. She learned early lessons about life's complexity from the area's distinctive blend of tradition and modernity; these were lessons she would later examine in her career as a journalist and broadcaster. Vanessa was well renowned for her precocity even as a young child. She had a passion for reading, mature conversation, and discussion. She was not afraid to voice her thoughts or raise concerns about the world.

Her viewpoint was significantly shaped by her Jewish roots as well. Her upbringing was centered on the Jewish ideals of social justice, education, and charity (tzedakah). Her family promoted a strong sense of identification and belonging by celebrating various Jewish customs and holidays. Vanessa felt anchored by this cultural background, but it also made her aware of the challenges of being a minority in a non-Jewish culture. Later in life, she would consider how her Jewish identity influenced her empathy and her willingness to provide voice to underrepresented groups.

Vanessa Feltz showed an unquenchable thirst for information from an early age. Her innate gift for words and her curiosity for the world were immediately apparent when she started school. Her early education was received at the esteemed independent Haberdashers' Aske's School for Girls in Elstree, Hertfordshire, which was renowned for its rigorous academic programs. Vanessa flourished in this setting, able to explore her passions for writing, reading, and debating.

Vanessa was not simply a conscientious student at Haberdashers'; she was an exceptional one. She soon became well-known for her exceptional aptitude in history and English, topics that enabled her to study human behavior, investigate narratives, and comprehend the intricacies of society. She also participated actively in the school's debate group, which helped her improve her public speaking and reasoning abilities. Her confidence was cultivated in this setting, which also helped her get ready for a career in journalism where her ability to think quickly and communicate clearly would be her defining traits.

Vanessa had a passion for reading that was evident from an early age. She read books nonstop, especially ones that questioned accepted wisdom or gave a thorough examination of the human condition. The writings of George Eliot, Charles Dickens, and subsequently Virginia Woolf captivated her. Their ability to portray the hardships and victories of common people struck a profound chord with her. Literature served Vanessa as a tool for comprehending the world and making sense of her personal experiences, in addition to being a source of entertainment. She would frequently look to books for comfort and inspiration, drawing from them the words and concepts that would further her own artistic goals.

Her academic accomplishments were not overlooked. Vanessa was accepted to study English literature at Trinity College in Cambridge. This was a noteworthy accomplishment, especially considering that women from Jewish backgrounds were still uncommon and Cambridge was still considered an elite university at the time. Vanessa was in the ideal setting at Cambridge, which has a long tradition of turning out some of the brightest minds in British literature, politics, and philosophy, to broaden her horizons intellectually.

Vanessa's time at Cambridge changed her significantly. She found herself surrounded by intellectuals, thinkers, and potential leaders at the university, which was a place of intense intellectual scrutiny. She flourished in this intellectually stimulating atmosphere, where discussions of politics, literature, and philosophy were commonplace. She was able to hone her critical thinking abilities and broaden her grasp of the expressive power of language during her time at Cambridge.

Vanessa received tutoring from some of the best literary minds of the day at Cambridge. She immersed herself in her studies, reading a ton and participating in the rigorous academic discourse that defined university life. She continued to hone her love of writing and storytelling there. Her understanding of the craft of writing and the power of words to captivate readers was further enhanced by her studies of great writers, including modernists like James Joyce and Shakespeare.

But for Vanessa, Cambridge meant more than simply academics. She also started to develop her own personality there, as a woman and a potential journalist. Being one of the minority of Jewish students at Cambridge presented challenges as well as opportunities for growth. She learned how to handle social settings where she was the outsider and it strengthened her sense of cultural pride. Later on, this experience would help her in her journalism, especially in terms of developing empathy for people who are marginalized in society.

Vanessa was also introduced to the media and journalism industry while attending Cambridge. Despite her literary studies, she found herself becoming more and more fascinated with the ways in which written language might enlighten, convince, and shape public opinion. She started composing opinion pieces and essays for several student magazines, covering a broad range of subjects from politics to culture. Her initial experience with journalism ignited a desire that would ultimately shape her professional path.

She learned early in her journalism career that words had the ability to alter perceptions, upend established wisdom, and effect social change. The notion that journalism could provide a voice to the voiceless particularly appealed to Vanessa, and this thought would recur throughout her career. Whether she was a radio hostess or a writer for major publications, Vanessa always tried to use her platform to speak to the concerns of common people.

Vanessa was certain she wanted to pursue a career in

journalism by the time she graduated from Cambridge. She was resolved to utilize her skills to change the world since she had come to strongly believe that words had the ability to influence public conversation. However, Vanessa faced difficulties along the way to become a journalist. During the 1980s, the media sector was primarily dominated by men, and gaining entry into it needed not only skill but also perseverance and resolve.

Vanessa started her media career after graduating from Cambridge by contributing to The Jewish Chronicle, where she developed her investigative and feature writing abilities. This early encounter had a significant influence on how she approached journalism. Her experience working for a Jewish-focused journal offered her a unique perspective on social justice, minority rights, and the value of giving voice to people who are frequently ignored by the mainstream media.

Vanessa's writing skills immediately attracted her attention, and she started contributing to national publications including Sunday Express and The Daily Mirror. Her popularity as a columnist stemmed from her ability to approach difficult subjects with wit and clarity. But it wasn't simply her writing that made her stand out; it was also her courage to defy expectations and take chances. Whether writing about pop culture, politics, or social issues, Vanessa always approached her subjects with a new viewpoint and an unapologetically honest voice.

Vanessa was steadfast in her belief that media should be a force for good during her early career. She approached every story with the belief that journalists had a duty to confront, inform, and educate their audience. Vanessa's art was marked by a fiery independence and a refusal to be hushed even in her early years. As she moved from print journalism to television and radio, these traits would come in handy and help her establish herself as one of the most famous voices in British media.

Vanessa Feltz was already building the foundation for an incredible journalism and broadcasting career in these early years of her career. Her schooling at Haberdashers' and Cambridge, along with her background in Islington, had equipped her with the mental fortitude and fortitude needed to excel in a demanding field. More significantly, they had given her a strong conviction that words have the ability to change the world, a conviction that would motivate her throughout her professional life.

CHAPTER TWO

The Rise of a Journalist

Vanessa Feltz's decision to enter the media field was more than just a professional move; it marked the start of a lifelong quest for the truth, a love of narrative, and a dedication to using her platform to raise social issues. Her journey began in the late 1980s, when males predominated in journalism and success took more than just skill—it also required a will to be heard. Vanessa's drive and the foundational experiences she gained during her time at Cambridge University influenced her early entrance into journalism.

Vanessa was eager to establish herself in the media after earning her degree in English literature from Trinity College, Cambridge. She had grown to have a profound passion for writing and a firm confidence in the ability of words to sway public opinion and bring about change. She started her career in journalism when she joined The Jewish Chronicle, a weekly publication that served the UK's Jewish population. This was a crucial point in her career because it was her official debut into journalism and it provided her with a forum to discuss topics that were important to her both personally and professionally.

Vanessa produced a range of items at The Jewish Chronicle, including opinion pieces, feature articles, and investigative reports. She developed her journalistic abilities here, realizing the value of thorough investigation, fact-checking, and the creation of gripping stories. Vanessa was able to create a distinctive voice by working for a community-oriented journal. This style blended audience sensitivity with a resolve to write about subjects that were frequently ignored in mainstream media. In addition to writing about matters pertaining to the Jewish community, she also addressed more general societal themes like social justice, race, and identity.

For Vanessa, working for The Jewish Chronicle was an amazing experience. Every journalist had to wear several hats in the small, tight-knit newsroom, which helped her become versatile in her writing and reporting. She had to overcome the difficulties of being a young woman in a field that was dominated by men, and she frequently had to put in twice as much effort to succeed. Vanessa remained resolute in the face of these obstacles. She was committed to making a name for herself in the media industry since she was confident in her abilities and motivation to achieve.

Vanessa's early work was notable for its combination of boldness and sensitivity while taking on challenging subjects. She treated every topic she wrote on, whether it was anti-Semitism, political events, or cultural changes within the Jewish community, with a keen understanding of the nuances involved. Her work at The Jewish Chronicle strengthened her conviction that it is crucial to give voice to individuals who are frequently disregarded and deepened her understanding of how marginalized communities are portrayed in the media.

Vanessa was also exposed to the difficulties of striking a balance between the demands of working within a particular community and journalistic integrity during her tenure at The Jewish Chronicle. Many of her readers relied on the newspaper as a reliable source of information about their neighborhood, so she had to walk a tightrope between telling it like it is and being sensitive to their feelings. When she moved into national media and had to balance the needs of a larger and more diverse audience, her early experience navigating the complexities of community journalism would come in handy.

Vanessa started contributing to other magazines, including as The Daily Mirror and Sunday Express, where her writing was recognized more widely, in addition to her job at The Jewish Chronicle. She immediately established herself as a perceptive, insightful journalist with a distinct viewpoint. She wasn't afraid to take a stand on things that others would avoid, and her essays frequently addressed contentious topics. She stood out from many of her contemporaries because of her openness to voice her opinions and her skill at writing with wit and clarity.

During this time, her writing demonstrated her increasing self-assurance as a journalist. Whether writing about social issues, politics, or culture, Vanessa always had a new, uncompromising voice. She realized that journalism was about creating stories that people could relate to, stories that could alter people's perspectives, provoke thought, and motivate action, not just gathering facts. This conviction that journalism has the ability to change the world would become a recurring motif in her work.

Vanessa's interest in the nexus between media and society grew as her work developed. She was aware that the media might affect public opinion and how people perceived the outside world. This was especially true in the UK during the 1980s and 1990s, a period of profound social and political transformation. Vanessa was determined to use her platform to engage with the public on problems that were at the forefront of debate, including gender discrimination, racial injustice, and the spread of multiculturalism.

The most noteworthy feature of Vanessa Feltz's journalism career to date has been her proficiency in opinion writing. Opinion writing enables journalists to go beyond the presentation of facts and discovery of truths, which is what reporting and investigative journalism are all about. Here, writers provide readers a viewpoint, interpret the facts, and help them navigate the complexities of a subject. Writing opinions has become Vanessa's way of questioning the existing quo and expressing her opinions on everything from politics to culture.

Although Vanessa started writing opinions pieces in her early journalism career, her real impact came from the national press. Her biting wit, unabashed voice, and incisive criticism shown her ability to engage readers in her columns in The Daily Mirror, Sunday Express, and other notable newspapers. She possessed a talent for dissecting difficult, frequently contentious topics in a way that was both understandable and thought-provoking.

Vanessa's ability to voice her opinions without fear of backlash distinguished her as an opinion writer. She didn't back down from contentious subjects or challenging discussions. Vanessa handled any topic she wrote on, whether it was social justice, gender inequity, or the shifting dynamics of British society, with courage and conviction. Her writing frequently reflected her own experiences, especially as a woman in a field controlled by men and as a Jew.

As an opinion writer, Vanessa excelled at fusing her own experiences with more general social comments. She was aware that the best opinion pieces are those that not only make a case but also engage the reader emotionally.

Anecdotes from her own life, such as her battles with body image, her experiences as a working mother, or her thoughts on relationships and love, were frequently included in her columns. Vanessa was able to connect with her readers in a manner that few other journalists could because she shared her own vulnerabilities with them.

Her writing remained serious despite this personal touch. Conversely, it helped to humanize and make her points more approachable. Vanessa have a special talent for taking the intimate and making it relatable. She discussed the difficulties of juggling work and family obligations, the demands placed on women by society, and the complexity of contemporary relationships in her writing. Many people could relate to these concerns, especially women who saw themselves in Vanessa's writing.

Vanessa's goal in penning her opinions was to provoke discussion rather than only provide analysis. She recognized that opinion writers had an obligation to interact with their readers, question their presumptions, and encourage them to think critically about the world they live in, and that journalism had the ability to influence public conversation.

Writing about popular culture, politics, or social issues, Vanessa always tried to elicit discussion and reflection.

Vanessa's keen sense of humor and scathing wit were two of the things that set her opinion writing apart. She frequently interspersed her pieces with sharp one-liners or amusing remarks, as she had a flair for using comedy to emphasize serious arguments. Her writing was both enlightening and amusing because of her ability to blend humor with serious analysis. Not only did her beliefs captivate readers, but her distinct voice—bold, unreserved, and refreshingly honest—drew them in as well.

Vanessa's strong sense of social justice and humanity were also evident in her work. She had a special passion for problems that marginalized populations, women, and minorities faced. She frequently addressed topics like racism, discrimination, and gender inequality in her writings, bringing attention to the injustices experienced by individuals who are marginalized in society. She urged readers to address these problems and fight toward a more just and equal society in her writing, which served as a call to action.

Vanessa never wavered in her belief that media should be a positive force throughout her career. She thought it was the duty of opinion writers to use their position to promote change and offer a voice to people who are frequently marginalized. Her literature, which continuously defended the rights of working-class people, minorities, and women, was a clear reflection of her belief. Vanessa's writing was always based on a strong dedication to social justice, regardless of the subject matter—politics, culture, or social challenges.

As Vanessa's career developed, penning opinions started to define who she was in public. She was well-known not just as a journalist but also as a pundit, and her readers looked forward to hearing her opinions on current affairs. Her articles frequently provoked strong reactions, sparking interesting discussions in the media and on social media. Vanessa was never hesitant to stir up controversy, but her writing was always motivated by a sincere desire to discuss the topics that her readers cared about most.

Vanessa's ability to engage her readers was a major factor in her success as an opinion writer. She realized that the greatest opinion writing was about striking up a conversation rather than giving a lecture or preaching. Her essays challenged readers to discuss her views, reflect critically on their own lives, and challenge preconceived notions. Vanessa's readers always knew that her work would entertain, challenge, and most importantly, make them think, regardless of whether they agreed with her. Her ascent as an opinion writer was, in many respects, a reflection of her larger career path as a journalist.

CHAPTER THREE

From Print to Screen

One of Vanessa Feltz's professional turning points was moving from print journalism to television. Although she was already well-known in print media for being a sharp and courageous journalist, her transition to television was what really shot her to fame. This was more than simply a professional move; it was a metamorphosis that would increase her fan base, change the way people saw her in public, and eventually establish her as a household brand in British media.

The UK's media environment was changing dramatically in the late 1980s and early 1990s. With more channels, more information, and a growing demand for individuals who could deliver insightful commentary and captivating entertainment, television was becoming a more and more potent medium. Vanessa was well-suited to enter this environment because of her wit, knowledge, and unwavering opinions. However, making the switch from print to television wasn't simple, particularly for a young woman working in a still male-dominated field.

Vanessa would soon learn that working in television requires a different set of abilities than working in print journalism. She had more time to formulate her ideas, hone her arguments, and polish her prose before it was printed. On the other hand, television required charisma, quick thinking, and immediacy. It was a medium in which personality counted as much as intelligence and where keeping an audience interested meant providing them with entertainment as well as information.

In the early 1990s, Vanessa made her television debut by doing guest appearances on a variety of discussion shows and news programs. She experienced what it was like to be in front of the camera during these early appearances, and she soon discovered that she had a natural flair for it. Her ability to think critically and talk clearly and convincingly about a variety of subjects made her an exceptional guest. After producers noticed, Vanessa soon had offers for more regular television employment.

Vanessa began her career in television as a presenter of The Big Breakfast on ITV. The show, a vibrant and irreverent morning show, was well-known for its lighthearted tone and ability to blend amusing entertainment with important news. Vanessa was supposed to be an interviewer and commentator on the broadcast, but she immediately won over the audience. She was a perfect fit for the format because of her ability to transition with ease between serious conversations and lighter moments.

Vanessa was able to show off her lighter side and develop her talents as a television presenter on The Big Breakfast. She gained knowledge on how to interact with a live audience, think quickly during interviews, and keep her cool in the frequently hectic world of live television. These abilities would come in very handy as she moved into higher-profile television jobs.

Vanessa's Big Breakfast success opened up a lot of other television opportunities. She started appearing frequently as a guest on programs such as Good Morning Britain and This Morning, where she was asked to talk about a wide range of topics, including pop culture and politics. Her ability to speak on a variety of subjects, along with her witty and straightforward demeanor, made her a highly sought-after pundit. Although Vanessa relished her role as a guest on these shows, she was aware that her real goal was to host her own show.

That chance arrived in 1994 when Vanessa received an invitation to host The Vanessa Show, an ITV chat show. The morning-tv program featured a blend of current talks, human-interest tales, and celebrity interviews. Vanessa's abilities as a journalist and a television personality were catered to by the format. She had the chance to interact with her audience, conduct in-depth interviews, and address the topics that were important to her, whether they were social justice, politics, or the difficulties of daily living.

The Vanessa Show became popular right away. The friendly demeanor, sharp mind, and affinity for connecting with both her speakers and her audience drew viewers in. She has the ability to humanize even the most somber subjects, and her interviews were frequently distinguished by their nuance and emotional resonance. Vanessa wanted to learn more about her guests' personal lives, including their goals, challenges, and victories. She wasn't only interested in petty celebrity rumors. This strategy helped her show stand out in a congested television market.

But Vanessa's move to television wasn't without its difficulties. She encountered her fair share of doubt and criticism because she was a woman in a field that was predominately male. Some questioned whether she could retain the same degree of intellectual rigor on screen as she had in print, while others questioned whether she had the appropriate "look" for television. But Vanessa, never one to back down, silenced her detractors. She was aware that substance was more important on television than just looks. And she soon dispelled any skepticism about her abilities with her perceptive mind and captivating demeanor.

Vanessa was different from other TV presenters, among other reasons, because she was genuine. Vanessa was a welcome change from the polished and scripted television personalities of today. She was not scared to be authentic on television and didn't put on airs. Vanessa was always real, whether she was sobbing, laughing, or questioning a guest's opinions. Because of her genuineness, she gained the respect of her viewers, who regarded her as more than simply a popular TV personality but as a person they could identify with—someone who wasn't afraid to be herself and voice her opinions.

Vanessa's profile was rising as The Vanessa Show gained more and more traction. She established herself as a mainstay on British television, garnering recognition for her astute analysis, captivating interviews, and audacious handling of challenging topics. Even while Vanessa was content with her achievements, she realized she could do better. She wanted to keep pushing the limits of what she could accomplish on television and challenging herself, not to just be a talk show host.

Vanessa took a risky step that would alter the course of her career in 1998 when she decided to leave ITV and join the BBC. Vanessa's career embarked on a new phase with her shift to the BBC, which was noteworthy in and of itself, given the network's prominence. With its long history of producing high-caliber journalism and programming, the BBC gave Vanessa the chance to broaden her horizons and tackle heavier, more difficult subjects.

Moving to the BBC wasn't risk-free for Vanessa. She was moving on from the security of her popular discussion show on ITV to a new and undefined position at the BBC. However, Vanessa saw the relocation as an opportunity to establish herself in a new setting. Although she was already well-known for being a competent and captivating TV personality, the BBC gave her the chance to demonstrate her abilities as a professional journalist and broadcaster.

Vanessa's daily television show, Vanessa, which broadcast on BBC One, was one of her first jobs at the BBC. The premise of the show was similar to that of The Vanessa Show, but it focused more on serious subjects and current affairs. Vanessa viewed this as a chance to learn more about the topics that were important to her, such as politics, social justice, and current cultural trends. She was committed to using her platform to address significant issues and spark thought-provoking conversations with her audience.

Vanessa was a hit, and she gained more credibility as a professional broadcaster. She gained notoriety not only as an entertainer but also for her keen mind and her dedication to taking on the problems that were reshaping society. Vanessa interviewed everyone with the same respect and curiosity, whether they were politicians, celebrities, or common people. She had a passion for delving into the core of stories, discovering what drove individuals and their aspirations.

Vanessa was able to take on a greater variety of assignments after joining the BBC. She started hosting radio shows, such as The Vanessa Feltz Show on BBC Radio 2 and then BBC Radio London, in addition to her daily television show. Vanessa had a new avenue to interact more personally with her listeners thanks to radio. The discussion, the sharing of ideas, and the bond between the presenter and the listener were what counted on radio, not the polished visuals of television.

Vanessa was a success in the radio industry. She was a fantastic fit for the media because of her quick wit, natural ability to connect with people, and ability to think quickly. Vanessa covered a wide range of subjects on her radio shows, including politics, pop culture, and private matters. Her invitation to call in and voice their opinions made the conversation lively and engaging. Vanessa soon made a name for herself as one of the most important voices on

British radio because to the enormous popularity of her radio shows.

Vanessa was able to pursue her passion for social justice and campaigning even more after moving to the BBC. She started contributing frequently to conversations about inequality, race, and gender, utilizing her position to draw attention to topics that the media frequently ignored. Vanessa had a special love for women's rights, and she frequently addressed topics like gender discrimination, domestic abuse, and the difficulties experienced by working mothers on her radio and television programs.

Vanessa's success at the BBC can be attributed in part to her ability to strike a mix between fun and serious news. She could switch from lighthearted bantering with her guests and debating tough political matters with ease. She became a darling among listeners and spectators due to her adaptability. She was more than simply a serious journalist; in one broadcast, she could make viewers laugh, cry, and ponder.

One of Vanessa's career turning points was her shift to the BBC. She was able to broaden her audience, take on more weighty subjects, and become recognized as one of the UK's most reputable journalists and broadcasters as a result.

CHAPTER FOUR

Vanessa the Person

Although Vanessa Feltz is well-known for her exciting career in radio, television, and journalism, the person behind the public image is equally, if not more, fascinating. Outside of the spotlight and microphone, Vanessa is a person who has experienced a rich and complicated existence that is full of heartache, personal victories, and periods of profound personal development. In order to really comprehend Vanessa Feltz, one must go past her achievements in her line of work and see the lady who has always made an effort to strike a balance between her professional obligations and those of her family, love, and personal wellbeing.

Having raised her two kids, Allegra and Saskia, with a strong sense of purpose and dedication, Vanessa is an incredibly proud mother. Being a prominent working mother, Vanessa frequently struggled to balance the demands of her job with her parental responsibilities. She has been candid in discussing the challenges of motherhood and the guilt associated with attempting to "do it all." Vanessa, though, has insisted that her girls are her greatest accomplishments despite everything. Allegra and Saskia have developed into accomplished women, and Vanessa's identity is fundamentally shaped by her role as their mother.

Vanessa has always placed a high emphasis on her family, and her Jewish background has greatly influenced the way she views the world and herself. Vanessa has talked a lot about the influence of her childhood, especially her parents' influence, whom she loved. Her mother Valerie was a homemaker, and her father Norman was a businessman. Vanessa has spoken of her upbringing as loving but challenging at times. Vanessa's views on body image and self-worth were greatly influenced by her mother's struggles with weight and low self-esteem.

Vanessa has never been one to keep quiet about the difficulties she has had in her personal life, especially when it comes to body image and the demands of being in the spotlight. She has had continual criticism over her beauty throughout her career, which she finds upsetting and painful. Vanessa's weight has received a lot of attention from the media, occasionally overshadowing her many achievements. However, Vanessa has always remained strong in the face of such criticism, sharing candidly about her struggles with weight and her path to accepting herself.

Vanessa has emerged as a strong proponent of body positivity in recent years, urging women to accept their physical selves and resist social pressure to meet predetermined ideals of beauty. She has become a relevant figure for many women who have had comparable difficulties because of her candor and honesty in sharing her problems. Because Vanessa's activism is based on personal experience, it has had an especially powerful effect. She utilizes her position to advocate for self-love and acceptance because she recognizes the emotional toll that body image concerns can have.

Heartache has certainly been a part of Vanessa's personal existence. She was married for 17 years to renowned physician Michael Kurer before their marriage terminated in divorce in 2000. Vanessa has been open about the emotional destruction she experienced throughout the very terrible time of her marriage ending. Due to the extensive media coverage of the divorce, Vanessa was forced to deal with the dissolution of her marriage in the public eye, which was awkward for her.

Vanessa walked out of the divorce stronger and more motivated than before, despite the grief. She immersed herself in her profession, turning to it as a coping mechanism for the emotional suffering. More significantly, though, Vanessa didn't let the incident define who she was. She has frequently stated that although her marriage ended in divorce, it also gave her invaluable lessons in tenacity, independence, and the value of pursuing happiness inside oneself.

When Vanessa met singer and former member of the musical group Phats & Small, Ben Ofoedu, in 2006, her life took an unexpected and happy turn. The two were inseparable very soon, and their bond grew into something really remarkable. Ben and Vanessa are almost ten years apart in age, yet they have always had a close relationship based on love, respect, and a sense of humor. Vanessa saw Ben as her second chance at love, and she has frequently talked about how the partnership has changed her life. Vanessa greatly enjoys the spontaneity and spirit of fun that Ben brought into her life. Being in a relationship with one of Britain's most well-known celebrity couples was not just a personal but also a public milestone for Vanessa. Together, they gave joint interviews, went to red carpet events, and told the world about their love story.

Ben, who is descended from Nigeria, also exposed Vanessa to other cultural experiences, which enriched her life and broadened her perspective. Vanessa has expressed her appreciation for their relationship's cultural interchange and how it has aided in her personal development. Together, Vanessa and Ben have successfully negotiated the difficulties that come with being in a well-known relationship, such as handling media attention and tabloid rumors.

Vanessa and Ben have been surprisingly open about their highs and lows throughout their relationship. They talked eagerly about their plans to get married and declared their engagement in 2007. The wedding, which has been the focus of a lot of media speculation, has not yet occurred. Despite their strong commitment to one another, Vanessa has always been honest about the reality that marriage isn't always their ultimate aim. For Vanessa, the significance lies not in the institution of marriage but in the connection itself.

Another example of Vanessa's capacity to welcome life with excitement and optimism despite her prior heartbreak is her relationship with Ben. Vanessa could have easily distanced herself from love following the anguish of her divorce. Rather than closing the door on happiness, she made the decision to keep an open mind, and that has made her very happy. The relationship between Vanessa and Ben serves as a reminder that happiness may be found at any time in life and that love can blossom at any age.

The public has always been quite interested in Vanessa Feltz's private life, which she has had to handle with poise and fortitude. Vanessa's romances, from her well-publicized divorce to her long-term partnership with Ben Ofoedu, have frequently made headlines in tabloid publications. Vanessa, meanwhile, has stayed unabashedly herself and hasn't allowed the media shape her story in any way.

Vanessa's excellent sense of humor is one of the reasons she has been able to remain true to herself despite intense public scrutiny. It's evident that her ability to laugh at herself and the silliness of fame has helped her get through some of the more trying times in her life. She has frequently claimed that humor is her best coping mechanism. Vanessa always finds the good in any situation, whether it's handling tabloid rumors or public conjecture about her personal life.

Vanessa has been cautious about how much of her private life she divulges to the public at the same time. She is honest and forthright about some parts of her life, but she also understands the need of establishing limits. Vanessa is aware that there are demands associated with being in the spotlight, but she has always been adamant about keeping control of her own narrative. She has made it clear that she believes it is important to keep some aspects of her life private, especially those involving her family and kids.

Vanessa has never hesitated to be herself, even in the face of the difficulties that come with being a public figure. Vanessa always speaks from the heart, whether she is discussing her relationship with Ben, her experiences as a mother, or her battles with body image. Over the years, her genuineness has won the hearts of a great number of people. Vanessa is one of the most relatable characters in British media because of her willingness to be open and honest with her audience about her challenges and victories.

Social standards about age, ethnicity, and romantic relationships have also been questioned by Vanessa's public partnerships, especially her one with Ben. Vanessa's relationship with Ben is evidence that she has never let other people's opinions to control how she lives. The media has frequently discussed their age gap, but Vanessa has always dismissed criticism, saying that love, not age, is what counts. Similar to this, talk has also been sparked by Vanessa and Ben's interracial relationship; nonetheless, Vanessa believes that love knows no bounds to race, culture, or social expectations.

Vanessa is an extremely admirable person who refuses to allow the opinions of others define her. She has always had an intense sense of independence in both her personal and professional lives. Vanessa has always remained loyal to herself, whether it's handling tabloid rumors or figuring out the intricacies of being in a public relationship. She isn't scared to live her life on her terms since she is confident in who she is.

Vanessa has talked in recent years about how crucial it is for her to find balance in her life. Vanessa has consciously tried to prioritize her personal life and wellbeing more after years of putting her profession first. She has talked on the value of self-care, including spending time with her family, taking time for herself, and just slowing down to appreciate the little things in life.

Vanessa's inner strength and perseverance are demonstrated by her capacity to keep her sense of self in the face of criticism from the public. She has seen her fair share of personal and professional setbacks, yet she has never wavered from her core values. Vanessa has always believed that authenticity—leading an honest, humorous, and deeply purposeful life—is the key to happiness. Because of her genuineness, she has become not only a well-liked personality in British media but also a successful journalist and broadcaster.

Vanessa Feltz is much more than just her public persona and professional accomplishments. She is a woman who has had a rich, colorful life full of joy, love, and a strong sense of duty to her family and morals. Vanessa is a person who exudes enthusiasm, humor, and heart whether she is on screen, in the radio, or just spending time with her loved ones.

CHAPTER FIVE

A Voice for Many

In addition to her work in journalism and television, Vanessa Feltz has been well-known for a long time because of her transparency about her personal challenges, which many can identify with, especially her struggles with weight and body image. Vanessa's weight reduction struggle and her dedication to body positivity have made her a significant and prominent voice for women who face similar issues in a world where physical appearance is sometimes overemphasized.

Vanessa has battled her weight since she was a small child. She was deeply affected by seeing her mother struggle with issues related to weight and self-worth as a child. She seen directly the profound effects that body image might have on one's emotional and mental well-being. Vanessa found herself constantly in the public eye as her media career took off and she entered adulthood. Particularly as a woman in television, where appearances are frequently examined far more closely than in other areas, the temptation to look a certain way was tremendous.

Vanessa carried the burden of society's expectations regarding her appearance for a long time. Her weight became a topic of public discussion and media criticism, which affected her emotionally. Vanessa, though, stayed strong despite all of the highs and lows. She chose to advocate for body positivity for herself and the many other women going through similar problems, instead of letting these demands shatter her soul. She realized that problems with body image had more to do with self-acceptance, mental health, and learning to love oneself despite external expectations than with weight or beauty.

Like many other women who have experienced a similar path, Vanessa has attempted a number of diets and exercise regimens in her personal life over the years. She was honest about the difficulties she had keeping up a healthy lifestyle and the frustrations she experienced when losing and gaining weight. Vanessa had psychological and emotional difficulties in addition to physical ones when trying to lose weight. She has talked about how her connection to eating was frequently linked to emotional solace and how challenging it may be to break free from that pattern.

Vanessa did not make the decision to get gastric band surgery lightly in 2019. It was a big decision. She underwent the procedure as part of her ongoing attempt to take back control of her health and wellbeing. Vanessa was open about her choice and acknowledged that surgery was a tool to help her reach her goals of a better weight and way of life. Above all, though, she was open about the reality that this wasn't a quick fix or a panacea. She went on to stress that losing weight is an extremely personal journey and that what is effective for one individual could not be for another.

Important discussions about weight reduction, surgery, and how people manage their health were spurred by her candor regarding the gastric band procedure and its effects on her life. In a world where celebrities frequently conceal or keep such sensitive decisions a secret, Vanessa's candor was welcome. She made it very apparent that getting medical assistance for managing weight is not a sign of weakness, particularly when done for the proper reasons—health, not social acceptance.

Vanessa's weight loss journey has, above all, always been centered on body positivity. Vanessa has continued to be a fervent supporter of accepting oneself, even following the procedure and her subsequent weight loss. She emphasizes that body positivity is about embracing and accepting yourself exactly as you are, regardless of whether you're trying to lose weight or not. It's not about reaching a specific size or weight. Vanessa's message is very clear: a woman's value is not determined by her size and shouldn't be based on her weight. Women of all shapes and sizes can relate to her support of body acceptance, especially those who have experienced marginalization or devaluation due to their looks.

Vanessa has a strong voice in a world where women are frequently unfairly criticized based only on their appearance. She has continuously reminded women that beauty comes in all forms and sizes and that they are more than just their physical appearance. Vanessa's struggles with weight and body image have made her a role model for others, demonstrating to them that these issues can be handled with grace, humor, and self-love.

Vanessa has a profound impact that goes well beyond body positivity. She has continuously used her voice to highlight larger societal issues that impact not only women but society at large and to advocate for women throughout her career. In her writing, radio broadcasts, and television appearances, Vanessa has discussed a variety of subjects, including social justice, gender equality, and the challenges that women confront on a daily basis.

Vanessa has made a strong case for gender equality and the recognition of women's contributions to society in all spheres of endeavor. Vanessa has worked in the media for many years, so she has firsthand knowledge with the difficulties faced by women in a field that is dominated by men. She has had to battle for her seat at the table, deal with misogyny, and endure sexism. She hasn't, however, given up or let these difficulties define who she is.

Vanessa has a very personal reason for supporting women. She recognizes the particular challenges faced by women, especially in the workplace, where it is frequently required of them to strike a balance between their home obligations and their professional aspirations. She has been outspoken about the challenges of being a working mother, the guilt that frequently follows attempts to strike a balance between career advancement and childrearing, and the discrimination that women experience in both their personal and professional spheres.

Vanessa has emerged as a significant voice in the discourse surrounding domestic abuse and the ways in which society may provide greater assistance to women who have experienced abuse. She has encouraged women to seek treatment if they are in violent relationships and has used her position to spread awareness of the warning signs of domestic abuse. Vanessa's work in this area is especially significant since it emphasizes that anyone may become a victim of domestic abuse, regardless of their financial situation or public reputation.

Vanessa has worked tirelessly to promote mental health awareness in addition to issues of gender equality and domestic abuse. She has been candid in discussing her personal battles with mental health, especially those with body image and self-esteem. Because of Vanessa's openness to talking about her own experiences, discussions regarding mental health are becoming less stigmatized, which encourages more people to ask for treatment. Her emphasis has always been on the value of therapy, self-care, and developing constructive coping mechanisms for life's stresses.

Vanessa is not just a professional advocate for women and society. She has always been a pillar of strength and encouragement for the women in her personal life. Vanessa has always been dedicated to uplifting people, whether it is by being a mentor to younger women in the media profession, helping friends get through tough times, or raising her daughters to be strong, independent women.

Vanessa's genuineness is one of the factors that makes her such a potent advocate. She connects with others by speaking from the heart and using her personal experiences as a springboard. Vanessa's comments have resonance because they are based on genuine, lived experiences, regardless of the topics she discusses—the difficulties of being a woman in the media, the demands of parenthood, or the significance of mental wellness. She is always willing to have the tough talks that need to be had, even if she doesn't claim to know everything.

Vanessa has also been an outspoken opponent of the stereotypes associated with aging in society, especially as it pertains to women. Vanessa has become more vocal as she has aged regarding the ways that society denigrates older women and the need to always look young. She has resisted these demands, preferring to accept her advanced age and cherish the knowledge and experience that go along with it. Vanessa wants women to know that growing older is a normal aspect of life and should be welcomed rather than dreaded.

Her support of women has not gone overlooked. For her work in the media and her services to society, Vanessa has won various honors and recognitions over the years. What matters most, though, is not the awards but rather the influence she has made on regular women's lives. Numerous women have been motivated by Vanessa to accept their bodies, speak out against injustice, and lead unapologetic lives.

Vanessa Feltz has had numerous positions in the public eye as a journalist, advocate, radio broadcaster, television presenter, and writer. But her strong desire to use her voice for good is at the core of everything she does. She has always aimed to question social conventions, push limits, and stand up for those who might not have a platform of their own. She has never been satisfied to just entertain or educate.

Vanessa left behind a legacy of fortitude, tenacity, and genuineness. She has handled life's ups and downs with dignity and humor, using both positive and negative experiences to better others. Vanessa consistently conveys a message of empowerment, whether it be about mental health, gender equality, or body positivity. She exhorts women to live their lives according to their own terms, to accept who they are, and to defy social constraints.

Vanessa is still a voice for many as she develops both personally and professionally. She has demonstrated that it is possible to be powerful, successful, and vulnerable all at once and that the source of true strength is being authentically yourself. As one of the most adored and significant public personalities in Britain, Vanessa has solidified her position by her activism, her integrity, and her will to improve the world. And in doing so, she has elevated herself beyond simply being a voice for many to that of a ray of hope and inspiration for future generations of women.

CHAPTER SIX

Criticism and Resilience

Vanessa Feltz has been the target of harsh criticism and scrutiny from the public and media throughout her career. Being a woman in the spotlight has presented difficulties, especially in the cutthroat and frequently cruel fields of journalism and television, where Vanessa has had to learn to live with constant scrutiny. She has endured everything, from criticism of her appearance to scathing assessments of her professional decisions, and she has emerged stronger on the other side.

Regarding her appearance, Vanessa has been subjected to criticism more often than not. Similar to several women in the media, Vanessa's physique and weight have frequently been the focus of public discussion. Her size has been the subject of several tabloid stories, some of which have been nasty and degrading. Early in her career, when society standards for women's beauty were much more strict and merciless, these criticisms were particularly harsh. The media was unrelenting in highlighting any changes in her weight, frequently reducing her achievements to conversations about her physique.

Vanessa has always responded to these attacks with incredible grace, even in the face of criticism. She never let the criticism define her or ruin her career, even though it was clearly devastating. Rather, Vanessa seized the chance to candidly discuss the demands made on women who are in the public glare. She opposed the idea that a woman's value should be determined by how she looks, and as a result, she rose to prominence as a body positivity champion. She has become a role model for women globally due to her reluctance to live up to unattainable beauty standards, demonstrating that success may exist without satisfying society's limited notions of beauty.

For her work in the media, Vanessa has also drawn criticism, especially for her audacious and outspoken nature. Whether it's on her radio shows, in her newspaper columns, or on television, she has never been afraid to voice her opinions. Vanessa has drawn criticism for her openness to voice her opinions in a media environment that frequently expects women to be submissive or compliant. Vanessa has received criticism for being "too opinionated" and "too brash," but she has never allowed such criticisms stop her.

In actuality, Vanessa's success in her work can be attributed in part to her candor. She doesn't hesitate to take on challenging or divisive subjects, and her straightforward style has won her a devoted audience. She has covered a wide range of topics over the years, including politics, social justice, and personal affairs, always with a special combination of wit, intelligence, and empathy. Even if not everyone shares her viewpoints, Vanessa's voice clearly speaks to a large number of people. Her unwavering individuality has contributed significantly to her long-term success.

Vanessa has also come under fire for switching from serious journalism to positions that were more entertainment-oriented. Vanessa gained recognition early in her career as a broadcaster and journalist, renowned for her astute observation and insightful interviews. But as her career developed, she stepped into more diverse roles, such as talk show host, reality TV star, and host of fun morning radio shows. She was criticized by some for allegedly "selling out" or losing credibility by moving away from the more scathing reporting she was well-known for.

But Vanessa has consistently disagreed with this story. She has been candid in discussing the value of changing with her work and refusing to be restricted to a certain kind of position. Vanessa's career in the profession can be attributed in large part to her adaptability. She has shown that being a serious journalist and an entertainer are both viable, and that one does not preclude the other. Despite the significant changes in the media landscape over the years, her career has remained vibrant and relevant due to her ability to adapt to many formats and audiences.

During her tenure as a presenter on the BBC's morning show "The Big Breakfast," Vanessa experienced a challenging beginning as she took over for the adored Paula Yates. This is arguably one of the most well-known instances of media criticism that Vanessa encountered. The adjustment was not well received by viewers, and the media jumped at the chance to capitalize on any perceived error. Due to low viewership, Vanessa eventually departed the show after just a few months. Vanessa found the experience tough because it was highly publicized and resulted in a lot of criticism, both personally and professionally.

Vanessa, meanwhile, refused to allow this failure define who she was. She has frequently discussed the things she took away from the event, most notably the value of resiliency and persistence. Vanessa stayed unwavering in the face of public scrutiny, persistently seeking out new chances and not letting one career setback deter her. She has been respected by both audiences and her peers for her capacity to overcome adversity, which has been a defining characteristic of her career.

Because the media is such a cutthroat industry, it takes a great degree of tenacity in addition to talent to survive in this highly competitive field. Vanessa Feltz has often shown that she possesses both of them. She has successfully negotiated the industry's frequent upheavals throughout her career, remaining loyal to her basic principles while adjusting to new audiences' tastes, technologies, and trends.

Vanessa's readiness to take on new challenges has contributed to her success in a field that is always evolving. She has never been one to settle for a role or rest on her laurels. Vanessa has always been willing to try new things, whether it was switching from print journalism to television or from serious news programs to lighter entertainment ones. Her capacity to adapt has helped her stay relevant in a field that is always changing.

Vanessa has gained popularity in the radio industry in recent years, especially thanks to her enduring morning show on BBC Radio 2. Vanessa now has a new opportunity to interact more personally with her listeners thanks to radio. Radio encourages more natural, unscripted conversations than television, where a large portion of the content is scripted or strictly controlled. Vanessa has flourished in this setting, interacting with listeners on a variety of subjects with her sharp wit, humor, and sincere empathy.

Her success in radio is evidence of her adaptability and tenacity. Vanessa has adapted to new formats while keeping her unique voice as the media landscape has changed, placing greater emphasis on digital platforms and streaming services. She has continued to be active on social media, interacting with her followers and keeping tabs on current events on sites like Instagram and Twitter. Vanessa has made sure that her profession is as exciting as ever by staying up-to-date and embracing new technologies.

Another example of her tenacity is Vanessa's ability to be true to herself in a field that frequently promotes conformity. Vanessa has never wavered from who she is, even when it hasn't always been the easiest course of action. Her ongoing appeal can be attributed in large part to her authenticity, as she has never attempted to fit into a template or be someone she is not. Vanessa is a popular choice among audiences because she is honest, candid, and doesn't back down from challenging subjects.

Vanessa has demonstrated remarkable personal resilience in addition to her professional resilience. Vanessa Kurer's 2000 divorce from him was a traumatic and widely reported event, but she came out of it stronger and more determined than before. She has been open about the emotional toll that her divorce took on her and how she turned to her work as a coping mechanism during that trying period. More significantly, though, Vanessa didn't let her marriage's dissolution to define her or make her feel less valuable. She showed that a person's struggles do not have to stop them from pursuing their work with the same zeal and determination.

Vanessa has demonstrated tenacity in her continuous struggle with problems related to her body image and the demands of being in the spotlight. Vanessa has been transparent about her challenges and used them as a platform to advocate for body positivity and self-acceptance, even in the face of persistent media attention regarding her weight. She has continuously defied social norms regarding what women should look like, and her courage to voice her opinions on these matters has elevated her to the status of a formidable voice for women everywhere.

Vanessa has had additional difficulties in the media profession as she has aged, mainly related to ageism. Older women who work in the television and radio industries frequently face discrimination and pressure to change or retire to remain relevant. Vanessa, however, has exceeded these predictions and has maintained a successful career far into her 60s. She has been outspoken in her support of accepting aging and opposing the idea that women lose value as they age. Vanessa's career serves as evidence that wisdom and experience are advantages rather than liabilities in the media industry.

Despite facing various criticisms, obstacles, and transformations, Vanessa Feltz has remained a consistent figure in the British media. Her ability to bounce back from setbacks and keep evolving in a field that is constantly changing is a result of her tenacity on both a personal and professional level. Vanessa is the same passionate, real, and funny person in everything she does, be it writing a newspaper column, presenting a morning radio program, or appearing on television.

What makes Vanessa unique is her capacity to adjust and flourish in the face of difficulty. Despite having experienced more than her fair share of hardships and criticism, she has never let them define who she is. Rather than giving up, she has made the most of every obstacle as a chance to improve, grow, and overcome. Not only is Vanessa's perseverance a personal quality, but it also defines her work and contributes to the reason that the British media continues to adore her.

One thing is certain as the media landscape changes: Vanessa Feltz's tenacity, authenticity, and unshakable commitment to being her true self will continue to help her adapt, thrive, and inspire others.

CHAPTER SEVEN
A Legacy Beyond Journalism

With good cause, Vanessa Feltz's name is linked with British media. She has established herself as one of the most identifiable and significant voices in the UK throughout the course of her decades-long career. Vanessa has had a career spanning many media, including print, radio, and television. Throughout it all, she has consistently combined humor, intelligence, and raw honesty. But Vanessa's contribution to British media transcends much more than her résumé of achievements. Her legacy is entwined with the development of contemporary British broadcasting, and her influence has been significant and far-reaching.

Vanessa has always been a trailblazer—from her early days in print journalism to her move to television. Vanessa was a welcome change of pace during a period when men predominated in the media, especially in prominent jobs. She demonstrated that a woman might be successful and even dominant in a field where women are frequently disadvantaged due to their gender. She broke down boundaries for other women in the media sector with her presence, especially in her early years. Vanessa showed that even in traditionally male-dominated environments, women could succeed as outspoken, aggressive, and intellectual voices.

The impact Vanessa had on British media cannot be overstated. Her distinctive style of broadcasting blended the earnestness and relatability of a talk show host with serious journalism. Her adaptability made it easy for her to move between different formats, whether she was talking about serious news stories, chatting with celebrities, or having lighter chats. Vanessa's ability to make her audience feel heard and noticed, though, was what really made her stand out. She had a true connection with her audience and listeners, and she had a remarkable capacity to speak on topics that touched people deeply on a personal level.

Vanessa's ability to bring traditionally "taboo" themes into the mainstream is one of her biggest achievements to British journalism. Vanessa has never shied away from talking openly about issues that the media frequently sidelined or overlooked, such as gender equality, domestic abuse, body image, and mental health. Vanessa's honest and frank discussion of these topics was crucial in altering the way the British media handled touchy subjects. Her readiness to address these issues, frequently utilizing her own life experiences as a foundation, made way for more open-minded and compassionate conversation on matters that have an impact on millions of people nationwide.

Apart from her contributions to journalism and radio, Vanessa has had a noteworthy influence on British culture in general. She has played a significant role in representing the Jewish community in the UK as a Jewish woman in the media. Vanessa has been outspoken about her Jewish background throughout her career, frequently sharing anecdotes and events that have molded who she is. Vanessa's exposure as a Jewish woman has been powerful and motivating for others in the community in a media landscape that has not always been varied. She has cultivated a more accepting and tolerant society by using her position to dispel myths and advance understanding.

Due to her extensive media experience, Vanessa has also been able to adjust to the changing British broadcasting scene. Vanessa has maintained her relevance in the media by embracing the shifts from traditional print and broadcast to digital and social channels. After making the switch to radio, she has had great success there with her BBC Radio 2 show. Because of the closeness of radio, Vanessa has been able to establish a more personal connection with her listeners. Millions of people tune in every day to her morning program because they enjoy her warmth, humor, and perceptive comments.

Beyond her professional accomplishments, Vanessa's genuineness has contributed to British media. Vanessa has stayed authentic all through her celebrity career. She has never wavered from her principles or attempted to conform to expectations set by the public or the industry. Vanessa's voice has consistently been genuine, unvarnished, and shamelessly honest—whether she's talking about weighty subjects or fun conversation. In a world of meticulously edited or staged media, Vanessa's genuineness is novel and, in many respects, revolutionary.

Generation after generation has adored her because of her approachability. One thing never changes: her relationship with the public, whether it be via "The Big Breakfast," her written essays, or later radio shows. Her audience found her. She is not only a well-known media character; viewers and listeners alike feel a connection to her. Because she opens up about her life to the public, including its highs and lows, weaknesses, and strengths, she has developed a strong relationship with the British people.

Another aspect of Vanessa's impact in British media is her influence and mentoring of the following generation of media celebrities, journalists, and broadcasters. Vanessa has fought for women in the media to speak up, take center stage, and be authentically themselves throughout her career. Numerous women have been inspired to follow in her footsteps by her, demonstrating that there are multiple routes to success in this field. Vanessa's career has shown that it is possible to succeed in the always changing media landscape while remaining true to oneself if one possesses these qualities: perseverance, hard work, and sincerity.

The legacy of Vanessa Feltz extends well beyond the media and journalistic industries. She has impacted the lives of innumerable individuals in the UK and beyond by using her platform to campaign for causes that are dear to her heart. Many people are deeply affected by Vanessa's influence, whether it is through her support of body positivity, her efforts to increase public awareness of domestic abuse, or her dedication to speaking out about mental health concerns.

Vanessa has made a huge impact on society by challenging conventional notions of beauty and advocating for body positivity. Vanessa has always been honest about her issues with weight and body image, and she has always advocated for acceptance and self-love through her platform. In a field that frequently places an extreme value on appearances, Vanessa has been a strong advocate against body shaming and unattainable beauty standards. Her candor regarding her experience losing weight, including her choice to have gastric band surgery, has contributed to de-stigmatize discussions about weight and body image, facilitating others' access to resources and support. Vanessa's message is very clear: self-worth should never be based on a scale number because beauty comes in all different forms and sizes.

In addition to her strong support of body acceptance, Vanessa has been a vocal champion for mental health awareness. She has been open about her personal battles with mental health, especially when it comes to the demands of being well-known. Vanessa has contributed to the reduction of stigma associated with mental health disorders by sharing her personal experiences and inspiring others to get assistance when they need it. Because so many people have been moved by her openness and sensitivity, she has become a significant voice in the continuing discussion around mental health in the UK.

Additionally, Vanessa's efforts to increase public awareness of domestic abuse have had a significant influence. She has spoken out on the warning signs of domestic abuse and the value of assisting survivors using her platform as a public figure. Her involvement in this field has been especially significant because it has helped bring attention to a problem that is frequently hidden. Vanessa has empowered victims of domestic abuse to come out and ask for assistance by using her voice to raise awareness, and she has inspired society at large to take this problem more seriously.

Vanessa has impacted society not only via her advocacy efforts but also through her interpersonal connections. She has served as an inspiration to her friends, family, and audience in addition to herself. Vanessa has always placed her family first despite the demands of her job, which have taken up a lot of her time and energy. She is a mother and grandmother. Her daughters have frequently mentioned how their own lives have been influenced by their mother's steadfast support, work ethic, and tenacity. It is evident that having a good career and a happy personal life are achievable because of Vanessa's remarkable ability to manage her demanding career and personal obligations.

Many have found inspiration in Vanessa's relationship with her long-term partner, Ben Ofoedu. After more than 15 years of dating, the couple's relationship has been characterized by love, respect for one another, and a common set of ideals. The relationship between Vanessa and Ben is proof of the strength of love and devotion, even in the face of criticism from the general public. Their partnership has demonstrated that genuine love can last, even in the spotlight, as they have traversed life's ups and downs together. Vanessa's life of influence is shaped by her experiences, her decisions, and her dedication to changing the world rather than by a single event or accomplishment. She has made positive use of her position by speaking out on important topics, standing up for people who might not have a voice, and encouraging others to lead genuine, unapologetic lives. Through her advocacy work, professional accomplishments, and interpersonal connections, Vanessa has had a lasting impact on the globe.

Her influence is felt not only in the media sector but also in the lives of all the individuals she has come into contact with. Vanessa has demonstrated that it is possible to have a prosperous profession, to handle hardship and criticism with poise, and to use one's position to change the world for the better. Her legacy is one of impact above all else, strength, resiliency, and sincerity.

Vanessa will undoubtedly continue to encourage and inspire people as her career develops. Her legacy includes a life lived with passion and purpose in addition to her professional accomplishments. She has become a true legend in British media and beyond by using her voice to advocate for people who might not have one.

CONCLUSION

In the British media, Vanessa Feltz has become well-known because to her talent at engaging audiences on a variety of media, including print, radio, and television. Although there have been difficulties along the way, she has always exhibited an unmatched degree of fortitude, tenacity, and genuineness. Vanessa Feltz's story is not only one of personal success but also one of the value of remaining loyal to oneself in the face of a business that can be cruel and harsh.

When we consider her remarkable career, it is important to recognize the subtleties that set Vanessa apart from her public character. She is not merely a TV personality or radio host. Vanessa is a symbol of bravery, openness, and a strong desire to build relationships. In today's media, her capacity to captivate listeners on topics ranging from the intensely personal to the blatantly political is exceptional.

Vanessa's ascent to popularity in the cutthroat world of British journalism is a tale of years of tenacity and hard work rather than an overnight success. Vanessa was raised in Islington, North London, and was influenced by books and language in her early years. Vanessa came from a family of scholars, and her education at esteemed schools like Haberdashers' Aske's School for Girls and later Trinity College, Cambridge, shaped her ingrained knowledge of politics, culture, and human feeling.

Her passion for expression, argument, and narrative was fostered by these early encounters. Her path to pursuing these hobbies led her to journalism, where she first gained recognition for her razor-sharp humor and unabashedly honest voice in print. In addition to providing her with a public platform, her work as an agony aunt and a writer for The Jewish Chronicle and Daily Mirror introduced her style, which is straightforward, approachable, and emotionally in touch with the lives of regular people.

Her foray into radio was not without its difficulties. It was not an easy undertaking to make the switch from print to screen, but Vanessa embraced it with the same dedication that has defined her whole career. Her time as host of The Big Breakfast in the 1990s demonstrated her innate talent for television, as her personality was evident on screen. Her engaging and personable qualities won over viewers right away. Vanessa started solidifying her status as a mainstay in British broadcasting at this time.

But when she entered the radio industry, her career took a more dramatic turn. Vanessa was able to interact more directly and personally with her listeners because of the intimate nature of radio. She became a beloved morning voice for millions of listeners when she moved from BBC Radio London to BBC Radio 2, where she provided warmth, wisdom, and humor. Radio, a medium that benefited from Vanessa's raw talks and candor, adored her for her ability to connect with her audience. One of Vanessa's greatest accomplishments is perhaps her influence on radio, which highlights her adaptability and steadfast bond with the British public.

Vanessa is well known for being a trailblazer for women in journalism and television, which is one of her greatest achievements to British media. Vanessa persistently dismantled obstacles in a traditionally male-dominated field. Her appearances on radio and television proved that, despite defying stereotypes perpetuated by the media, women could be intellectual, powerful, and authoritative in public.

Vanessa refused to comply to the standards of beauty or opinion associated with her gender, nor did she rely on projecting the image of the stereotypical female television presenter. She approached difficult talks with bravery and fearlessness. Vanessa didn't just take part in the conversation; she frequently took the lead, whether it was on delicate subjects like gender equality or delicate subjects like domestic abuse. Her support of women was revolutionary, especially when it came to her candor regarding the demands of the media and the criticism of her appearance. Vanessa successfully fought against the tabloid culture's fixation on looks and weight, introducing body positivity to the mainstream media.

Her openness regarding her personal weight loss experience, including her choice to have a gastric band surgically placed emphasis on her vulnerability while also demonstrating incredible bravery. Vanessa made it possible for people to realize that it was acceptable to struggle and that getting help—whether for mental health or body image—was a sign of strength rather than weakness. She opened the door to discussions that were previously forbidden.

Vanessa has fought for people who frequently feel ignored by using her position to advocate throughout her career. She has spoken out against issues like mental health, domestic abuse, and the pressures women experience in society. Vanessa was able to establish a degree of trust with her audience by utilizing her personal experiences as a framework. This allowed her to fill in the blanks in conversation about challenging subjects.

Being a well-known Jewish woman, Vanessa has also utilized her platform to promote understanding and fight anti-Semitism. Her public persona has always highlighted her Jewish identity, and she has never held back when talking about her background, religion, or the prejudices she has encountered. Others in the Jewish community have benefited from this transparency, which has helped to mainstream conversations about religious identity and cultural pride.

Her impact goes beyond her professional life. Younger journalists and broadcasters, especially women, have been motivated by Vanessa to pursue their dreams of success without compromising their morality or sense of self. Her legacy will go on for many years to come because of her commitment to guide and support newer talent.

Although Vanessa has achieved great success in her career, the public has also shown admiration and intrigue for her personal life. She has faced many difficulties, one of which was her highly public divorce from Michael Kurer in 2000. Vanessa came out of this traumatic event stronger than ever, refusing to let it destroy her profession or her sense of self. Her openness about her personal issues made her even more relatable to her audience. She has frequently talked about how her profession provided her a sense of purpose during this trying time.

The public has also been captivated by Vanessa's long-term partnership with musician Ben Ofoedu, which is a tale of love, dedication, and cooperation. In a world where negativity is often the norm in the media, Vanessa and Ben's relationship has provided a welcome example of respect and encouragement for one another.

Vanessa leaves behind a complex legacy. She has had a major influence on the British media scene as a journalist. She paved the path for later female generations in journalism and broadcasting by demonstrating the value of knowledge, sincerity, and vulnerability in a field that frequently rewards superficiality. She has used her platform to start important dialogues about gender equality, body positivity, and mental health awareness.

However, Vanessa's relationship with her audience is possibly her greatest legacy. She has always been more than just a journalist or broadcaster; to millions, she has been a dependable confidante, friend, and source of consolation. Vanessa is one of the most adored characters in British media because she has always been able to connect with people on a human level, whether through her radio shows, television appearances, or written essays.

Vanessa Feltz's narrative will endure as an inspiration to tenacity, genuineness, and the importance of keeping loyal to oneself throughout her professional journey. Many others have been uplifted, challenged, and inspired by her journey, and her legacy as an incredible journalist, advocate, and person will go on for years to come.

Printed in Great Britain
by Amazon